Establishing a Foundation

Career Planning Blueprint for Leaders Overview

The Career Planning Blueprint for Leaders Workbook helps you build plans for improving and marketing your brand elements in order to increase your likelihood of obtaining a promotion.

In this guide you will:

1. Capture Educational and Practical Experience
2. Validate Your Knowledge, Skills, and Abilities (KSAs)
3. Develop a Career Succession Plan
4. Identify the Scope of Your Desired Roles
5. Identify Three Types of Advisors
6. Identify Career Gaps
7. Develop Various Action Plan

This special leadership guide also includes a section on:

- The Katz Model

CAREER PLANNING

BLUEPRINT

CREATE YOUR OWN SUCCESS

LATRICE COLLINS

THE CAREER BRAND
for
PROFESSIONALS

ISBN 978-0-9660-451-6-1

Table of Contents

Career Brand Overview

Your ability to excel in any career (whether you are working as an entrepreneur or working for someone else) is primarily based on how well you demonstrate your career brand. We have created a career brand model that consists of four elements: Expertise, Image, Character and Impact. Each element answers a specific question every hiring manager needs answered when deciding who to place in a position.

The Career Brand Model

Element	Question
Expertise	What do you know?
Image	How will you represent me?
Character	How do you fit with me?
Impact	What will do for me?

To discover your career brand, we have created a powerful web-based brand evaluation tool that provides you with a comprehensive review for how you and others see your personal career brand. Visit www.WhatsMyCareerBrand.com.

Types of Advisors

It will be important to identify one or more proven professionals to help and advise you during this journey. These should be people you respect. There are three types of advisors to consider.

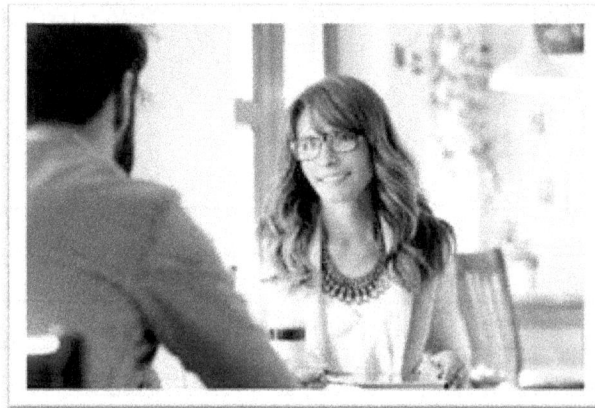

Mentor:

A mentor is an experienced person who is willing to provide guidance or advice in a particular area. A mentor may or may not be in a position of power or authority. This person provides their services free of charge.

Sponsor:

A sponsor is typically a person in a position of authority or power. You have proven to them that you possess particular strengths. A sponsor often speaks highly of you when you are NOT in their presence and works behind the scenes to position you for promotion or career advancement opportunities. You typically do not ask a person to be your sponsor. This role, in some cases, grows out of the mentor role. It is the result of the positive growth demonstrated in the sponsor's eyes. This person provides their services free of charge.

Coach:

A coach is typically a paid role. Typically, a coach and a mentee have a specific goal they are looking to accomplish. The coach provides guidance, direction, and measurable tools. They typically require an action plan. The coach will hold the individual accountable to completing the plan, and course-correct as they move toward the predefined goal.

Identify Your Areas of Opportunity and Your Advisors

It's recommended that you have multiple advisors. No one person is exceptional at everything. Consider your area of interest.

- Some people have great moral and ethical compasses
- Some are great salesmen
- Some are great technicians (they can fix any problem)
- Some are great people-managers
- Some are great influencers
- Some have taken career journeys you wish to follow.

Important

Just be careful to be clear on what specific attribute you are seeking from each individual. For example, a person may be a great technician, but not the greatest people-manager. Hence, you WOULD ask this person's advice on job-related items, but you WOULD NOT ask for their advice on human issues.

For best results, be sure to select advisors who have a moral compass and values that are similar to or better than your own. Your beliefs are your foundation. Guard your virtues wisely.

Advisor's Name	Area of Interest	Type of Advisor
		o Mentor o Sponsor o Coach
		o Mentor o Sponsor o Coach
		o Mentor o Sponsor o Coach
		o Mentor o Sponsor o Coach

Self-Discovery

Before you can build a strategy for your career and personal growth, it's important to identify your starting point in each area. This book allows you to identify your strengths and areas of opportunities. This section will cover three important categories for leadership roles:

1. Practical Experience
2. Knowledge, Skills and Abilities
3. Technical, Conceptual, and Human Skills

Practical and Education Experience

For some reason, some people claim to have experience because they are familiar with a concept, or because they took a topic in school, or have watched a person do something before. On the contrary, practical experience means YOU HAVE DONE IT BEFORE. You have walked in those shoes. You understand the pain points associated with the roles. You have had successes and failures and know what to look out for that a person without experience might not.

Have you ever had a person who had never raised a child tell you how to raise one? Have you met a person who had never managed an employee, but told you how easy it is to do? These individuals may have theoretical experience, i.e., they understand from afar, but they have not actually done it before.

Practical Experience

There is power in your practical experience. Use the chart below to list your experiences.

Specific Experience	Number of Years

Advanced Education

List your education including college degrees, licenses, certifications, and awards.

Specific Education	Year Completed

Licenses, Certifications, and Awards	Year Completed

Knowledge, Skills and Abilities

Most forward-thinking people have an array of skill sets, which sometimes makes it that much more difficult for them to narrow the focus. Complete the questions that follow to help you laser- focus on your attributes..

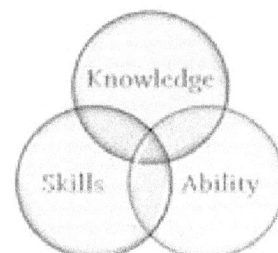

Knowledge:

Knowledge is described as what you specifically know regarding a particular topic.

Questions to ask yourself:

- What do you know about your craft?
- What do you know about your company?
- What do you know about your industry?
- What do you know about your competition?
- How does your knowledge differ from that of others?
- How does your knowledge help your employer, future employer or customers?

Skills:

Skill describes what you can do.

Questions to ask yourself:

- What can you do when it comes to your craft?
- What can you do when it comes to working with people?
- How do your skills differ from those of others?
- How do your skills help your employer, future employer or customers?

Abilities:

Ability describes your talents, special skills and aptitudes.

Questions to ask yourself:

- What natural abilities do you have? For example, do you learn faster than others?
  Do you have a talent for persuasion? Can you calm down a hostile customer?
- How do your abilities differ from those of others?
- How do your abilities help your employer, future employer or customers?

Discovery Your KSAs Activity

Use the table below to create your list of knowledge, skills and abilities (KSAs).

My Knowledge (Things I Know)	My Skills (Things I Can Do)	My Abilities (My Natural Talents & Attributes)

The Katz Leadership Model

If you are interested in either a management role or becoming your own boss, the Katz model is a great tool to help you understand the scope of skills needed for the role you wish to obtain.

Robert Katz created the Katz model of leadership in 1955. He proposed that all employees require some level of technical, human, and conceptual skills. The following diagram is an illustration of the Katz model.

The next few pages will provide additional information on the Katz model and help you to identify your specific skill level.

TECHNICAL SKILLS

These skills refer to the knowledge you have in your role and your proficiency in a specific type of work or activity. The "technical skills" category becomes less important as you increase your level in management. Technical does not mean technology (though it can, if that is your profession). It's about the details necessary to complete work effectively.

When thinking about your technical skills, ask yourself a few questions:

- What are all the things you know regarding your role or industry?
- What are all the things you can do in regards to your role or industry?
- Which skills do you have that are superior to those of most people in your field?
- What is your knowledge of the laws that govern the role?

Write Your Technical Skills Below

#	My Technical Skill(s)
1	
2	
3	
4	
5	
6	
7	
8	
9	
10	

HUMAN SKILLS

Human skills refer to how well you work with people – how well you adapt, flex and blend with others to form solutions, and how effective you are at building relationships. This group of skills is the second-largest in the first-line manager role. They are the most significant skills needed for middle managers.

For middle managers, this is their primary responsibility. They are the people difficult decisions and complaints are escalated to. A middle manager is the liaison between the staff and senior management. This role is also responsible for influencing multiple teams to work as one. Managers who have not proven themselves to have strong human skills have a difficult time being promoted into middle management.

Senior management represents the face to the public, investors, regulatory agencies and the employees. However, these interactions are less frequent than the human interactions of the middle managers. Therefore, human skills are the second-most important skill for the top levels of leadership.

When thinking about your human skills, ask yourself a few questions:

• How well do you manage relationships?
• What skills have you mastered for influencing people?
• What is your proof you have strong human skills?

Write Your Human Skills Below

#	My Human Skill	What levels of the organization were involved?
Sample	Key leader assigned to resolve critical customer satisfaction issue linked to high emotions, financial errors and organizational risks.	Front-line employees, peers, numerous departments, senior executives, customers
1		
2		
3		
4		

CONCEPTUAL SKILLS

Conceptual skills represent the ability to create ideas and concepts. These skills require vision and strategic thinking. Conceptual skills are the most important skills in top management. Businesses that lack leaders with conceptual skills often fail because they do not stay ahead (or with) competition and the changing times.

When thinking about your conceptual skills, ask yourself
a few questions:

- What ideas that you've suggested have been implemented?
- Who benefitted from your idea (just you, your team, the customers, and/or the business)?
- What was the impact of your idea(s)?
  o How much money did it save the company?
  o What efficiency was improved?
  o Did it help the customers?

Write Your Conceptual Skills Below

#	My Concepts and Ideas	Who was impacted?	How was the impact measured?
Sample	Change the process for notifying customers of billing to an e-notification	Company Customer	Saved $15,000 in shipping and postal fees. Provided stronger service to the customer
1			
2			
3			
4			
5			
6			
7			
8			

How do you determine your level?

Consider the skills you have identified. Compare them with the chart below. Place an "X" in the box that corresponds to your ACTUAL skill level. To check your self-assessment, ask a leader you respect (see the Advisor section later in this manual) to review your analysis and validate you have rated yourself effectively.

	Conceptual	Human	Technical
Senior Management	Responsible for moving organization forward. Focuses on changes in the industry and technology as well as customer's needs and interests.	Responsible for high-profile or critical relationships necessary to run a business. Major relationships include business partners, investors, bankers, regulators, media, and department executives.	Responsible for high-profile or critical relationships necessary to run a business. Major relationships include business partners, investors, bankers, regulators, media, and department executives.
Middle Management	Responsible for identifying methods for improving efficiency and impact for the larger area. Thinks more broadly than their group and identifies ways to grow or advance across business lines.	*Connects to senior management, line management, employees and customers. Responsible for solving disputes and leading staff.*	Understand the general items related to your line of business. Aware of how larger groups fit within the organization.
First-line Management	Recommends and implements ideas to improve function of their team's role. May also implement solutions for their line of business or their customer base.	Connects to peers, employees and customers. Responsible for solving disputes and leading staff.	Aware of how their team connects into the general flow of the organization.

Example

You were promoted into the role of supervisor two years ago due to your expertise. You now lead a team of five people. You are respected by your team and you are heavily involved in your team's activities. You are intimately familiar with all the functions, and you are still seen as the subject-matter expert for your area. You have not developed other team members to become managers because, frankly, no one does the job as well as you do. The company has also employed one or two of your ideas to improve efficiencies.

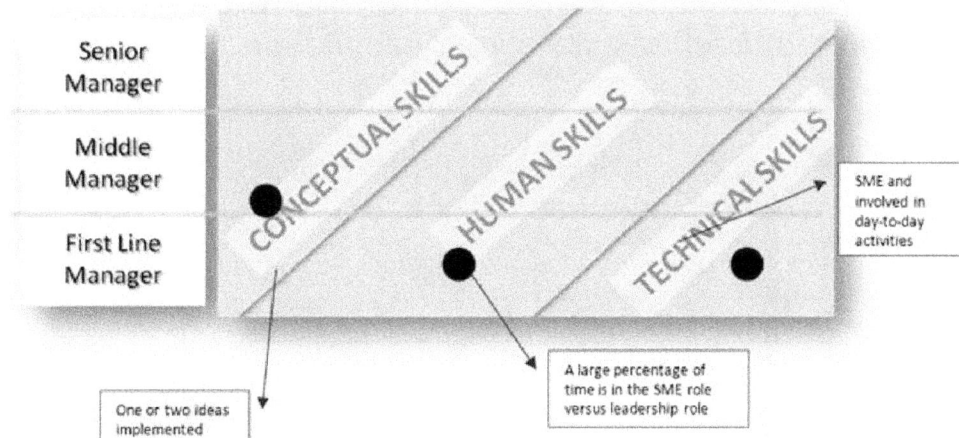

DISCOVERY

The individual above is a strong asset to any company. He ensures production is maintained and employees are valued. His experience qualifies him to be a supervisor or in a manager role. If he aspires to be considered for middle management (director, vice-president, etc.) it is important for him to shift his focus. His lack of developing his team has two impacts:

1. A large amount of his focus is in the technical realm. The over-focus on he technical component of the job is limiting him from showing his expertise in developing more conceptual solutions.

2. Middle managers are responsible for moving the entire team forward

with measurable results.

The middle-management role is more strategic and less technical. Middle managers have strong team members who execute the technical aspects of their role. Allowing the employees the ability to focus on the technical aspects of the job frees the manager to work on other human and conceptual skills.

Your Turn

Review the chart below. Identify the scope of your experience and place a dot in each area that best describes your experience, then self-analyze your findings.

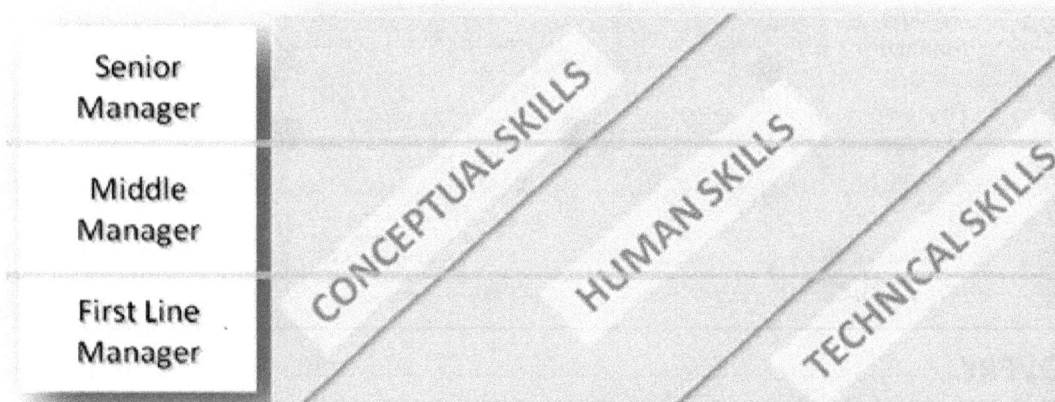

Self-Discovery

Analyzing Your Readiness
for Future Role(s)

Building Your Career Succession Plan

Your growth and advancement in life is your responsibility. No one recognizes your desires and passion for life better than you, nor can anyone dictate the path you should travel.

This section is designed to provide clarity on your short- and medium-term career and personal goals. Since each experience helps pave the way for your future, this model only lays out plans for two levels of promotions. After navigating through your career path, you are encouraged to revisit your strategy and build additional future goals.

Use the next few pages to identify the types of roles you want. Then review your skill sets to determine what you will need to position you for the role. Use the Career Succession Plan templates to build your strategy.

Succession Plan Draft

Careers can take twist and turns. However, most people have an idea of potential paths they can take. See the example below.

1. Working from the bottom up, write down your current role
2. List three realistic and possible next roles
3. List the next possible roles.

Sample

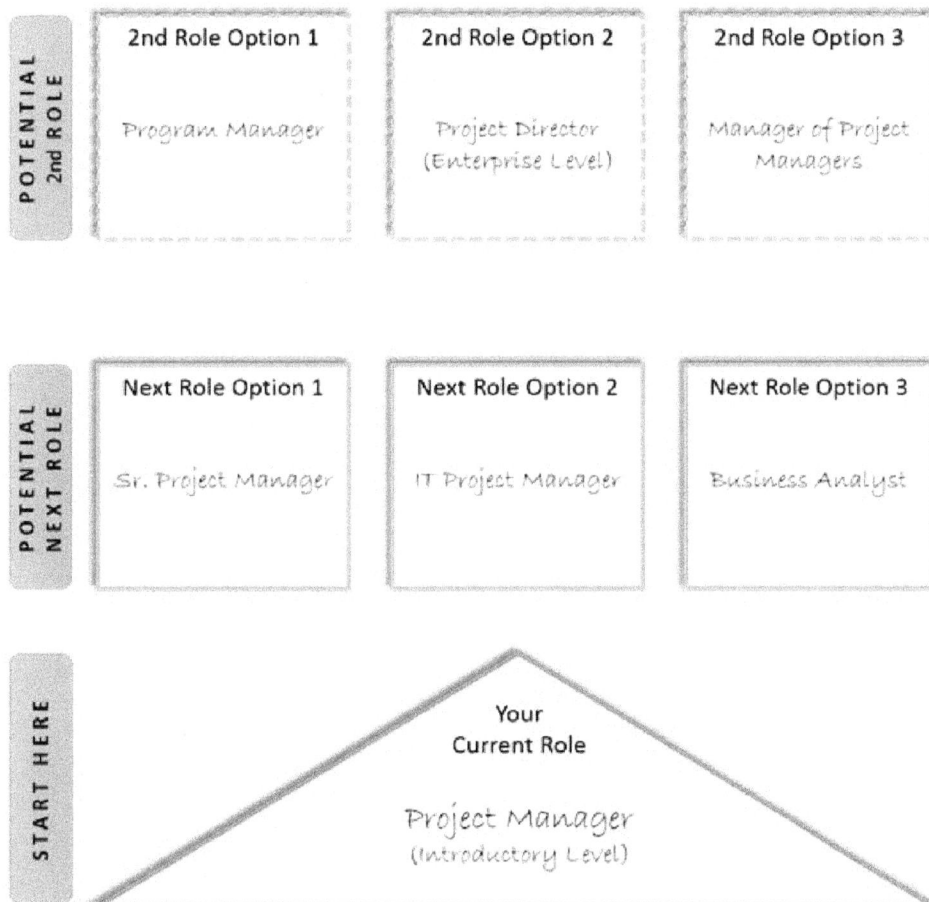

Succession Plan Draft

Now you try.

Think hard about the types of roles available to you. Think outside the box. Remember, sometimes it is good to make a lateral move to give you experience you may need in various areas.

Instructions:

1. Working from the bottom up, write down your current role
2. List three realistic and possible next roles
3. List the next possible roles.

POTENTIAL 2nd ROLE	2nd Role Option 1	2nd Role Option 2	2nd Role Option 3

POTENTIAL NEXT ROLE	Next Role Option 1	Next Role Option 2	Next Role Option 3

START HERE	Your Current Role

Career Succession Planning

Career planning involves setting a career goal and implementing a strategy for obtaining it. Below, you begin to develop your career strategy. On the left side of the page, list your desired role. Under the role, identify all the major Knowledge, Skills and Abilities (KSA) needed for the role. On the right side of the page, list actionable steps for obtaining each promotion.

Role:

Write the Must-Have Criteria Below: (Education, Direct Experience, Licenses or Certificates)

☐ _____

☐ _____

☐ _____

Place a check in the boxes of criteria you have already obtained.

Key Knowledge, Skills, and Abilities

What skills do you have to prepare you for this role?

- _____
- _____
- _____
- _____
- _____
- _____
- _____
- _____
- _____

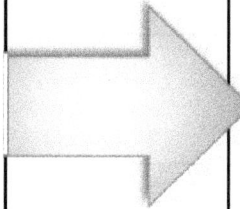

Strengths: Which KSA on the left have you mastered?

- _____
- _____
- _____
- _____

Opportunities: Which KSA on the left do you need to grow in to master?

- _____
- _____
- _____
- _____

What did you discover about your readiness to obtain this position?

Technical Skills	Human Skills	Conceptual Skills

Work with one or more advisor to assist you in identifying the gaps in the role you are interested in obtaining.

Advisor's Name	Gaps	Level of Gap
		o Mentor o Sponsor o Coach
		o Mentor o Sponsor o Coach
		o Mentor o Sponsor o Coach
		o Mentor o Sponsor o Coach
		o Mentor o Sponsor o Coach

Level of Gap

Critical:	(Major Gap)	This is a required attribute in order to qualify for the role.
Important:	(Large Gap)	This is a necessary attribute to successfully perform in the role.
Minor:	(Minimal Gap)	This is a small gap but may be relevant to the hiring manager for the role.

Career Succession Planning

Career planning involves setting a career goal and implementing a strategy for obtaining it. Below, you begin to develop your career strategy. On the left side of the page, list your desired role. Under the role, identify all the major Knowledge, Skills and Abilities (KSA) needed for the role. On the right side of the page, list actionable steps for obtaining each promotion.

Role:

Write the Must-Have Criteria Below: (Education, Direct Experience, Licenses or Certificates)

☐ _____

☐ _____

☐ _____

Place a check in the boxes of criteria you have already obtained.

Key Knowledge, Skills, and Abilities

What skills do you have to prepare you for this role?

- _____
- _____
- _____
- _____
- _____
- _____
- _____
- _____
- _____
- _____

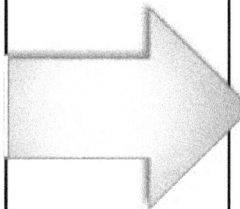

Strengths: Which KSA on the left have you mastered?

- _____
- _____
- _____
- _____

Opportunities: Which KSA on the left do you need to grow in to master?

- _____
- _____
- _____
- _____

What did you discover about your readiness to obtain this position?

Technical Skills	Human Skills	Conceptual Skills

Work with one or more advisor to assist you in identifying the gaps in the role you are interested in obtaining.

Advisor's Name	Gaps	Level of Gap
		o Mentor o Sponsor o Coach
		o Mentor o Sponsor o Coach
		o Mentor o Sponsor o Coach
		o Mentor o Sponsor o Coach
		o Mentor o Sponsor o Coach

Level of Gap

Critical:	(Major Gap)	This is a required attribute in order to qualify for the role.
Important:	(Large Gap)	This is a necessary attribute to successfully perform in the role.
Minor:	(Minimal Gap)	This is a small gap but may be relevant to the hiring manager for the role.

Career Succession Planning

Career planning involves setting a career goal and implementing a strategy for obtaining it. Below, you begin to develop your career strategy. On the left side of the page, list your desired role. Under the role, identify all the major Knowledge, Skills and Abilities (KSA) needed for the role. On the right side of the page, list actionable steps for obtaining each promotion.

Role:

Write the Must-Have Criteria Below: (Education, Direct Experience, Licenses or Certificates)

☐ _____
☐ _____
☐ _____

Place a check in the boxes of criteria you have already obtained.

Key Knowledge, Skills, and Abilities

What skills do you have to prepare you for this role?

- _____
- _____
- _____
- _____
- _____
- _____
- _____
- _____
- _____

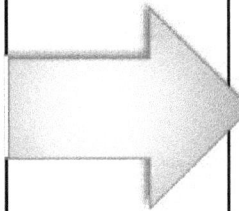

Strengths: Which KSA on the left have you mastered?

- _____
- _____
- _____
- _____

Opportunities: Which KSA on the left do you need to grow in to master?

- _____
- _____
- _____
- _____

What did you discover about your readiness to obtain this position?

Technical Skills	Human Skills	Conceptual Skills

Work with one or more advisor to assist you in identifying the gaps in the role you are interested in obtaining.

Advisor's Name	Gaps	Level of Gap
		o Mentor o Sponsor o Coach
		o Mentor o Sponsor o Coach
		o Mentor o Sponsor o Coach
		o Mentor o Sponsor o Coach
		o Mentor o Sponsor o Coach

Level of Gap

Critical:	(Major Gap)	This is a required attribute in order to qualify for the role.
Important:	(Large Gap)	This is a necessary attribute to successfully perform in the role.
Minor:	(Minimal Gap)	This is a small gap but may be relevant to the hiring manager for the role.

Career Succession Planning

Career planning involves setting a career goal and implementing a strategy for obtaining it. Below, you begin to develop your career strategy. On the left side of the page, list your desired role. Under the role, identify all the major Knowledge, Skills and Abilities (KSA) needed for the role. On the right side of the page, list actionable steps for obtaining each promotion.

Role:

Write the Must-Have Criteria Below: (Education, Direct Experience, Licenses or Certificates)

☐ _____

☐ _____

☐ _____

Place a check in the boxes of criteria you have already obtained.

Key Knowledge, Skills, and Abilities

What skills do you have to prepare you for this role?

- _____
- _____
- _____
- _____
- _____
- _____
- _____
- _____
- _____

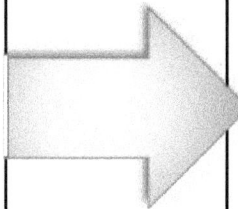

Strengths: Which KSA on the left have you mastered?

- _____
- _____
- _____
- _____

Opportunities: Which KSA on the left do you need to grow in to master?

- _____
- _____
- _____
- _____

What did you discover about your readiness to obtain this position?

Technical Skills	Human Skills	Conceptual Skills

Work with one or more advisor to assist you in identifying the gaps in the role you are interested in obtaining.

Advisor's Name	Gaps	Level of Gap
		o Mentor o Sponsor o Coach
		o Mentor o Sponsor o Coach
		o Mentor o Sponsor o Coach
		o Mentor o Sponsor o Coach
		o Mentor o Sponsor o Coach

Level of Gap

Critical:	(Major Gap)	This is a required attribute in order to qualify for the role.
Important:	(Large Gap)	This is a necessary attribute to successfully perform in the role.
Minor:	(Minimal Gap)	This is a small gap but may be relevant to the hiring manager for the role.

Creating Your Succession Plan Timeline

Succession Plan Timeline – Sample

1. Using the top boxes, transfer the gaps you identified in the previous templates.

2. Write the specific action you will complete to bridge your gap under the "How" header.

3. If you identified an advisor, use the bottom boxes to list the advisor's name and the skill they will help you develop.

4. To strengthen your plan, add dates by which each item is to be completed and draw a line from the box to the date on your timeline.

Gap	**Gap**	**Gap**	**Gap**
No Management Experience	Lack of experience with understanding how departments work together	Very low report development skills	Personal Refinement & Grooming
Action?	**Action?**	**Action?**	**Action?**
Serve as Relief Manager	Volunteer for stretch projects	Take Advanced Excel courses	Expand wardrobe; get manicure and pedicure twice per month

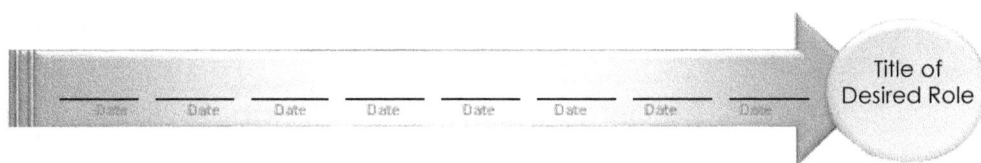

Date   Date   Date   Date   Date   Date   Date   Date

Title of Desired Role

Advisor	**Advisor**	**Advisor**
Jane Doe	Jeff Malinski	N/A
On What?	**On What?**	**On What?**
Managing groups and personal emotions	Exposure to understanding company perspectives	N/A

Succession Plan Timeline

1. Using the top boxes, transfer the gaps you identified in the previous templates.

2. Write the specific action you will complete to bridge your gap under the "How" header.

3. If you identified an advisor, use the bottom boxes to list the advisor's name and the skill they will help you develop.

4. To strengthen your plan, add dates by which each item is to be completed and draw a line from the box to the date on your timeline.

Gap	Gap	Gap	Gap
Action?	Action?	Action?	Action?

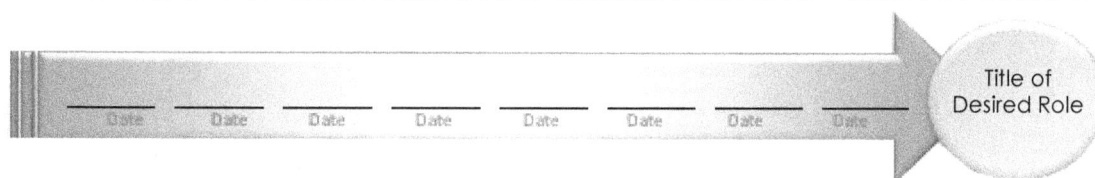

Date Date Date Date Date Date Date Date → Title of Desired Role

Advisor	Advisor	Advisor
On What?	On What?	On What?

Succession Plan Timeline

1. Using the top boxes, transfer the gaps you identified in the previous templates.

2. Write the specific action you will complete to bridge your gap under the "How" header.

3. If you identified an advisor, use the bottom boxes to list the advisor's name and the skill they will help you develop.

4. To strengthen your plan, add dates by which each item is to be completed and draw a line from the box to the date on your timeline.

Gap	Gap	Gap	Gap
Action?	Action?	Action?	Action?

Date — Date — Date — Date — Date — Date — Date — Date → Title of Desired Role

Advisor	Advisor	Advisor
On What?	On What?	On What?

Succession Plan Timeline

1. Using the top boxes, transfer the gaps you identified in the previous templates.

2. Write the specific action you will complete to bridge your gap under the "How" header.

3. If you identified an advisor, use the bottom boxes to list the advisor's name and the skill they will help you develop.

4. To strengthen your plan, add dates by which each item is to be completed and draw a line from the box to the date on your timeline.

Gap	Gap	Gap	Gap
Action?	Action?	Action?	Action?

Date Date Date Date Date Date Date Date

Title of Desired Role

Advisor	Advisor	Advisor
On What?	On What?	On What?

Succession Plan Timeline

1. Using the top boxes, transfer the gaps you identified in the previous templates.

2. Write the specific action you will complete to bridge your gap under the "How" header.

3. If you identified an advisor, use the bottom boxes to list the advisor's name and the skill they will help you develop.

4. To strengthen your plan, add dates by which each item is to be completed and draw a line from the box to the date on your timeline.

Gap	Gap	Gap	Gap
Action?	Action?	Action?	Action?

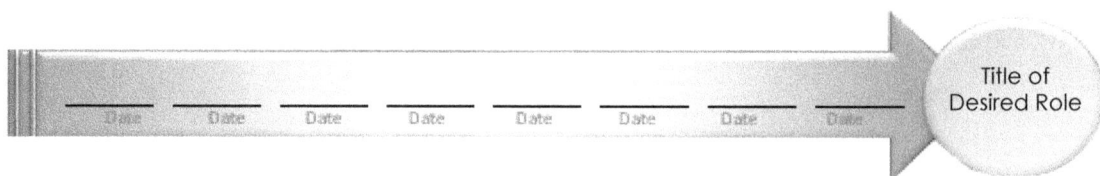

Date   Date   Date   Date   Date   Date   Date   Date → Title of Desired Role

Advisor	Advisor	Advisor
On What?	On What?	On What?

Accomplishments

Sometimes it looks like you've made little accomplishments, just because you have not achieved one or more of your goals. Every few weeks or so, use the space below to write down your accomplishments. This will help you look back and see just how much you have grown and accomplished in a very short period of time.

Accomplishment	Date

www.ingramcontent.com/pod-product-compliance
Lightning Source LLC
Chambersburg PA
CBHW062109090426
42741CB00015B/3377